I0800861

Table of Contents

Foreword

Helen Alvaré

There is almost certainly nothing so exciting and so mysterious in the course of our human lives as the process by which our Creator knits together inside of a mother an entirely new human being — a *particular* human being sent to this man and this woman to love and nurture. It is at once a very private event for the parents — coloring nearly their every thought from the first moment they learn of it — and an inescapably public one.

The world often treats the time of pregnancy as it treats the time of engagement: as an occasion for urging the couple to buy every conceivable need and want, or for warning the couple to organize their entire future, insofar as time and money are concerned.

The Church knows, however, that it doesn't matter whether your baby has the most elaborate crib or the simplest one, or even whether the mother and father have managed to foresee and provide for juggling their future work and financial responsibilities. First and foremost is the fact of this gift of a new son or daughter, which by itself dwarfs anything a woman could receive at a baby shower. Through the miracle of God's design, the parents' act of love brings them a new life — a life who links the mother to the father in an irreplaceable way, and who links the mother's family to the father's, and old relatives to young, with a force that takes them all by surprise, and provokes further gifts of love between them. Even non-family — neighbors, parishioners, co-workers, and friends — are receiving a gift from the new parents: the sweetness and innocence of a child among them, a reminder of how much we humans depend upon one another, a "vote of confidence" that the world is a place with a future, and the transformation of a man and a woman into a mother and a father, who by caring for their children come to care more about the communities and the planet we all share. Children bring nothing less than all this to the world. If this seems like overstatement, imagine a world with few or no more children. What an expression of failure and hopelessness that would be!

This booklet is a gift to expectant parents. It is about taking a moment, amidst the excitement of a pregnancy, to thank God for the gift of your child, to place your child in God's loving care, and to remember that your child is a gift to the world.

GIFT OF JOY

The Blessing of the Child in the Womb

Archbishop Joseph E. Kurtz and
Msgr. J. Brian Bransfield

Our Sunday Visitor Publishing Division
Our Sunday Visitor, Inc.
Huntington, Indiana 46750

18 17 16 15 14 13   2 3 4 5 6 7 8 9

ISBN: 978-1-61278-723-7 (Inventory No. X1433)

Cover and Interior Design: Amanda Falk

Cover Artwork:
Kissing the Face of God
© Morgan Weistling, courtesy of The Greenwich Workshop, Inc.

"Kissing the Face of God"

Introduction

No Ordinary Joy

The abundant love of Jesus Christ is the inexhaustible source of all life. The first and fundamental of His gifts is the gift of new life when a mother conceives a child. The presence of new life in the womb of the mother brings unique joy and hope to the center of our families, our Church, and our world. It is never too early to give thanks for the gift of new life and to ask the Lord for His blessing. The Rite for the Blessing of a Child in the Womb is a special moment to ask God for His blessing and to be a witness to the absolute wonder of the gift of new life.

A gift does not have *to do* anything. The *mere presence* of a gift can make a child's eyes double in size. The gift, hiding beneath a thin layer of wrapping paper as the mysterious package sits on a table during a birthday party or under the tree on Christmas morning, *ignites something* in the child. The decorative paper, held in place by a colorful bow, simply doesn't stand a chance before the wildly beating heart of the child. His or her eyes widen even more as the paper tears and falls away and he or she reaches for the gift itself.

SHUTTERSTOCK

We are, perhaps, most familiar with the standard custom of exchanging Christmas gifts and birthday gifts. However, to understand the true meaning of "gift," we have to go even deeper. Often, because of our regular practice, the giving of a gift at Christmas or on a birthday or special anniversary can come to be expected or even take on the nature of a transaction. However, the phenomenon of a birthday gift or a Christmas present can help remind us of the deeper meaning and possibility of a true gift.

Still, there is more to the original meaning of a gift. A true gift is something – or even some*one* – we would never have expected. A true gift is sheer and absolute generosity. It is without charge; it cannot be controlled. A true gift is beyond our power and cannot be confined. No conditions can be set on a true gift. Gifts bring joy and happiness. The happiness from a gift reaches our heart and shapes our spirit. As we grow up, we might lessen the intensity with which we tear through the paper, but we never outgrow the love for the gift.

God, too, loves to give gifts. Long before a young child ever *receives* a birthday gift or Christmas present, he or she *is* a matchless and unrepeatable gift. The child is not a reward, trophy, or prize. The child is a gift. How wondrous when the gift is a person! We all stand — parents, especially so — in complete receptivity and thankfulness before God's gracious gift of the life of the child in the womb.

The gift of human
life must always be given the utmost respect.

The first of all of God's gifts is the *gift of life*. You are reading this book because God has bestowed on you, or someone close to you, the gift of new life. When a man and a woman come together as husband and wife, they make a gift of love to one another. This love is unlike any other. It is total: they share themselves completely. God has decided that the gift of life, when it does emerge, should do so in and through the love of the mother and father. Even when a man and a woman without the benefit of marriage conceive a child, they are called to recognize their child as a gift. The Church is exceedingly eager to welcome you warmly, accompany you graciously, and care for you tenderly in your call to be a mother or father. God has given you the gift of life. Yet, if we look closely at this mysterious gift, we see a second one immediately: At the very same moment when God created your child, He also created you as a mother and as a father. Christ rejoices with you in this new moment.

SHUTTERSTOCK

Christ, in and through His Church, wants to celebrate the gift of life that God has given to you. You might attend church weekly, or perhaps you attend monthly, or only at Christmas and Easter. You may be distant from the Church, and perhaps you did not expect to be back at Church at all. No matter what may stand in the way between you and God, you and His Church, it is not worth holding you back any longer. This is a new moment, *a new beginning*, and Christ calls you to enter more deeply into the life of the Church and the regular practice of your faith. The gift is already unfolding. Nothing can stand in the way of the gift. The LORD Jesus tells us that He alone makes "all things new" (Rv 21:5). Your child has, along with God, given you a gift — and an *invitation* — and a blessing for your parish and for society at large.

Jesus is so excited about the gift of life that He gives a special blessing for this gift. The *Rite for the Blessing of a Child in the Womb* was approved on the solemnity of the Immaculate Conception, December 8, 2011, by the Congregation for Divine Worship and the Discipline of the Sacraments at the

Vatican. The Spanish text of the blessing received approval the following March. The United States Conference of Catholic Bishops promulgated the blessing for use in all U.S. dioceses on the solemnity of the Annunciation, March 26, 2012.

This special blessing is meant to be received one time at some point during the pregnancy. The mother simply has to approach the pastor of her parish to inquire about arranging for the blessing. The blessing can take place within the celebration of Holy Mass or outside of Mass. In fact, a group of expectant mothers and fathers can receive the blessing at once, together. While envisioned to be a public moment, the blessing can happen with as few or as many participants as is deemed proper, even simply between the individual mother and the priest. The blessing of the child in the womb is above all a pastoral moment: it is the first time that the child is evangelized and is a time of new evangelization for the parents, family, and friends. The blessing warmly extends the love of Jesus Christ as a family prepares for the birth of a child. At the same time, this sacred gesture can serve to announce, in a hope-filled way, the marvelous gift of human life and to encourage preparation for baptism.

This book consists of four short chapters. The first chapter helps to guide parents to understand the invitation to the unique vocation as Christian mothers and fathers. The second chapter explains the importance of the Rite for the Blessing of a Child in the Womb. The third chapter describes the role of your parish at this moment. Finally, the fourth chapter focuses on the contribution to all of society that you make as a mother and father. Several short questions are found at the conclusion of each chapter. The questions are meant either for personal reflection or for group discussion, whichever you prefer.

God is moving in your life in a remarkable way. He now offers you an invitation and a blessing. In His great plan, He also offers this invitation to your parish and society. Let's turn first to the invitation.

A SPECIAL NOTE: Some of you reading this book may have experienced the deep pain of losing a child in the womb. Some of you may also have experienced the pain of infertility or know others who are hoping to conceive and give birth but are having difficulties doing so. Jesus reaches out to you, aware of the unique and intimate suffering these experiences bring. The Church is grateful for those in the medical profession who seek to assist wives and husbands in ways that respect the gift of life and the dignity of conjugal love. For those who have lost a child or continue to have difficulties conceiving, may the Lord grant you His consolation and hope. In the midst of your suffering lived in Christian hope, you remain powerful witnesses to the gift and sanctity of new life. May your witness lead others to reverence that gift. Another moment of pain and difficulty is when the father of the child is unwilling or unable to accept responsibility for the spiritual welfare for his child. In such circumstances, the heroic love of the single mother becomes a special gift to the child.

Shutterstock

Chapter One

The Invitation

Your child is a new creation. The first news of new life is an instant of immeasurable astonishment and wonder. The first thing the Blessed Virgin Mary did when she learned she was to be the Mother of God, and that she carried the Lord in her womb, was to share this good news with her relative, St. Elizabeth. The Gospel tells us Mary went "in haste" to tell Elizabeth (see Lk 1:39). Elizabeth herself was pregnant with St. John the Baptist. In fact, Elizabeth's joy at the news that Mary shared was so deep and profound that John the Baptist *leapt* in Elizabeth's womb. When Elizabeth heard Mary's greeting, the infant in her womb "leaped for joy" (Lk 1:41-44). In a similar way, you have undoubtedly felt the deep amazement and profound wonder of God's presence at work in the mystery of new human life.

We often do not give enough time to our amazement. The wonder can quickly yield to innumerable hectic tasks and much activity, and even anxiety for couples preparing for the birth of a child. Certainly, there are many important things a couple must *do* when they learn they are expecting a child. Priorities shift quickly. In fact, the news of the child in the womb can often be a time of great concern and care as the mother and father seek to do all they can to care for the new human life and prepare for a healthy and safe delivery. We should never neglect or put off these important tasks. But expectant mothers and fathers are invited to something more than just the *doing*. The period of waiting is an *opportunity*. The invitation is, as you carry out all the crucial and vital tasks associated with preparing for birth, to allow the wonder and amazement to be the center and catalyst of everything else you must do. Otherwise, hurry, stress, and anxiety can begin to take over.

SHUTTERSTOCK

Certainly, a mother and a father are at their *busiest* during pregnancy and when their child is born. They are also at their *best*. The Rite for the Blessing of a Child in the Womb helps to deepen the mystery of the gift and beauty of new life. Your child is a living invitation to always keep the gift at the center of everything you do during the time of pregnancy and beyond.

In our culture, we really need to hear the warm and beautiful message of the Rite for the Blessing of a Child in the Womb. So much of our daily life is spent *earning*. There is something noble about *earning*. An industrious spirit leads us to make positive contributions to society as we study well, work hard, and earn a living. Yet, so easily, even this busy and productive lifestyle, so important to the workplace, finds its way into our relationships with family and friends. We can begin to run our family as if it were a business. Commonly enough today, the widespread contemporary mindset is that we expect profit and are entitled to immediate returns on anything we may do. In this attitude, we can easily begin to judge our family and friends on the feelings or experiences they produce for us. This brings untold tension and stress to places that are meant for joy and acceptance.

We forget that, though they often require work and effort, family and life are *gifts*, not jobs. We never tire of reaching out for the gift because a gift brings a *special, unordinary* joy. A gift is free; it cannot be earned.

And so, there are many new tasks before you as you prepare for the birth of your child. You most likely have started to make lists of all the significant duties and responsibilities now before you. Close family and friends are eager to assist. As all this goes on, remember that you are being invited to *deepen your life on a variety of levels.* You are bringing a new life into the world and so many people are happy for you and eager to celebrate with you this time of joy!

Certainly, news of the gift of your child is a most personal moment, but it is not a private moment. It is a public moment: a moment that your family, your parish family, the entire Church, and all of society want to share and celebrate warmly with you. Joy grows and deepens when it is shared. People are probably acting differently around you. They may spend more time with you or assist you with various things. This is because the presence of your child in the womb and your joy at this moment is a *sign* for so many people, a sign of hope and new life. The world *needs* and is drawn to this beautiful sign of hope and life.

Every gift is in some way also an invitation.
So, too, the gift of your child is an invitation.

Your child is already offering you an invitation. He or she is inviting you to see the meaning of life in a new way. The conception of a child is a call to a new responsibility for you as a mom or dad — to embrace your vocation as a Christian mother and father in the "formation and transmission of the Christian faith from the very beginning of life."[1] Your special vocation as parents means that you have a special mission: the primary mission you have received from God is to share your faith with your child.

SHUTTERSTOCK

Sometimes today parents delay the baptism of the child. This is often a less-than-conscious decision and, in fact, happens as a kind of "non-decision." Perhaps they are afraid or embarrassed to approach the Church because they have been away from the practice of their faith. Or, perhaps they are so busy that they prioritize other things, and they never arrange the baptism. Then, when they do think of it, they are self-conscious about approaching a priest for baptism because the child may be older now. No matter what reason holds you back, please consider seeking the baptism of your child. This is precisely why Jesus, in and through His Church, *longs to reach out with deep affection and kindness.* Nothing can separate us from the love of Jesus Christ for His people offered enthusiastically in and through His Church. *God never tires* of reaching out to renew His life within us. Your vocation as a Christian mom and dad is too important to let anything stand in the way.

Through you, your child is also offering an invitation to your fellow parishioners. They unite with you in joy and expectancy for the birth of your child. Today is the day to contact your parish pastor and begin to share the great invitation that is already forming at the center of your life. A central way to do this is to join with the Church in celebrating the Rite for the Blessing of a Child in the Womb. Today is the day to be like the Blessed Mother and to proceed to share the good news of God's life and love with those who long to assist you in your vocation and mission. Today is the day to share your amazement and wonder at God's new creation: the gift of your child.

1 Synod of Bishops, XIII Ordinary General Assembly, The New Evangelization for the Transmission of the Christian Faith, *Instrumentum Laboris* (Vatican City: 2012), 111.

Questions for Personal Reflection or Discussion

1) Think about how it feels when you or a loved one is expecting a child. How might you keep these feelings of wonder and amazement alive in your daily life?

2) Feelings of amazement and joy are natural and healthy, but some people can become overwhelmed with the necessary preparations for the baby. Even though some activities are very important during the time of pregnancy, what are some ways someone who is expecting a child can prevent busyness from blocking the deeper meaning of new life?

3) What images come to mind when you think of the vocation and mission to be a Christian mother and father?

Shutterstock

Chapter Two

The Blessing

In the first chapter we discussed the presence of Jesus in the womb of the Blessed Mother, which is the first thing the Gospel tells us about Jesus. The last thing Jesus does in the Gospel before He ascends to His Father after the Resurrection is to bless His Church (see Lk 24:50). A blessing is important. Throughout the Bible, a blessing shows forth the generosity of God. The first thing God does after creating man and woman is to bless them. This first blessing is also a calling, a summons: "Be fertile and multiply; fill the earth and subdue it" (Gn 1:28). A blessing is therefore never something one keeps for oneself. It is a sacred moment in which God designates a person and sets him or her aside for God's special purpose and gifts.

DesignPics

A blessing is also a reminder that the abundant good gifts we have received come ultimately from God. In the Bible, God promises His people the blessings of life (see Gn 27:28), strength (Gn 27:29; 49:8), land (Gn 27:28; 27:39; 49:9), and children (Gn 15:5; 48:16; 49:8). God is always generous, even though in times of trials, such as what Job experienced in the Old Testament (Jb 1-2), we can find it most difficult to understand His ways. As noted in the introduction, some readers may have undergone the painful experience of losing a child or of not being able to conceive. Some may be going through a difficult pregnancy now. These experiences are hard to understand and can bring great suffering. In faith and trust, we know that the grace and mercy of God accompany us through these difficulties, even when clear answers are not available. Our Lord Jesus showed us this trust in the Father most especially on the Cross. Even in sorrowful times, God is close to us. He lovingly holds you and your child close to His Sacred Heart.

A blessing is not magic. It is not superstition. Most of all, God's blessing is never simply a one-time ceremony, but emphasizes a never-ending relationship renewed every single day.

A blessing *uncovers* and makes clear the gift of God in this present moment. A blessing ceaselessly points to and reminds us of something. A blessing does not remind us in a nostalgic way, but in a way that actually makes God's action present in our lives here and now, today. A blessing reminds us of the most important thing in life. It reminds us *to live a holy life,* a life bonded to God by means of His holy covenant with us fulfilled in His only Son, the LORD Jesus Christ.

This is why a blessing is said to sanctify us or make us holy: *the blessing places God at the center* of the life of the one who is blessed. Therefore the one who is blessed *now becomes a sign* to strengthen others in the most important journey we will ever make: the search for and journey to God. The blessing does not begin or end with us. It begins in God and leads us back to God. It is given to us *for others*, for society and the Church. The one who receives a blessing also receives, at the same time, a call and a summons, a vocation. He or she has now become a great *reminder of God* for everyone. A blessing leads us back to God – to worship God, in particular, by attending Sunday Mass each week, receiving the Sacrament of Penance on a regular basis, and through daily prayer. Simply put, a blessing has two directions. First, God's generous action comes down upon us, and second, our thanksgiving and devotion ascend to God.

The Rite for the Blessing of a Child in the Womb is an important part of your lives of faith as a mom and a dad. The blessing is an opportunity for you to share the gift of new life and the invitation to amazement at this new life. While the reality of a blessing is truly rich, arranging for it can be very simple. A blessing ordinarily takes the form of words and gestures pronounced over the person to be blessed. The order and sequence of these special words and gestures is called a "rite." If an expectant mother and father decide they would like to arrange for the child in her womb to receive the blessing, the first step is to contact the pastor of the parish and set a time to discuss preparation and arrangements for the details of the celebration of the blessing. As noted, the ceremony of blessing itself can be as reserved or as public as the mother and father desire. Arrangements can be made for the blessing to take place during the celebration of Mass or outside of the celebration of Mass. Family, friends, and neighbors, indeed any of the faithful or persons of good will, can easily be invited. It can take place in church or, for specific pastoral reasons, in another suitable location.

SHUTTERSTOCK

How appropriate is a blessing in this time of hope and excitement. It provides a rich opportunity for support and prayers. Of course, just as there is the external preparation for the blessing, there is an internal preparation. This is a wonderful time for you as a mom or dad to begin to pray more frequently and, if you have not been doing so up to now, to attend the Sunday celebration of the Eucharist each week. God longs to share the depths of His mystery with you. He longs to bless you.

This rite itself is contained in a small book entitled *Rite for the Blessing of a Child in the Womb*. When the time for the blessing arrives, after all is prepared and arrangements are complete, ordinarily the priest or deacon will gather everyone, make the Sign of the Cross, offer a greeting, and invite everyone to prayer. After a reading from sacred Scripture, it is typical for the celebrant to invite the mother to step forward, along with the father, and even some other family members if this is fitting. He then extends his hands in a gesture of blessing and says these words:

God, author of all life,
bless, we pray, this unborn child;
give constant protection
and grant a healthy birth
that is the sign of our rebirth one day
into the eternal rejoicing of heaven.

LORD, who have brought to this woman
the wondrous joy of motherhood,
grant her comfort in all anxiety
and make her determined
to lead her child along the ways of salvation.

For the father:

Lord of the ages,
who have singled out this man
to know the grace and pride of fatherhood,
grant him courage in this new responsibility,
and make him an example of justice and truth for this child.

For the family:

Lord, endow this family
with sincere and enduring love
as they prepare to welcome this child into their midst.

Lord, You have put into the hearts of all men and women of good will
a great awe and wonder at the gift of new life;
fill this (parish) community
with faithfulness to the teachings of the Gospel
and new resolve to share
in the spiritual formation of this child in Christ our Savior,
who lives and reigns for ever and ever.

Amen.

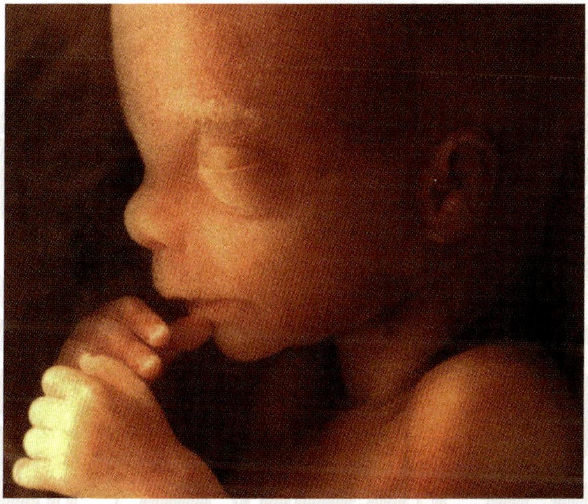

BrandX

Those are the powerful words that mark the special blessing for the child in the womb. These words really and truly call down, at the time of the blessing, the action of God to bless the child. God, through His Church, *begins* something with this blessing. God begins to draw even closer to the child in the womb, to his or her mother, father, and family, and to the entire parish.

SHUTTERSTOCK

The Rite for the Blessing of a Child in the Womb is not the same as the Sacrament of Baptism. The Blessing for a Child in the Womb, while it can be the first step in preparation for your child's baptism, is a separate moment that comes before baptism. The blessing *cannot* replace baptism in any way; rather, the blessing *points to* and begins to get us ready for the Sacrament of Baptism. It is very important during the time of pregnancy to begin to prepare for your child's baptism, in which your son or daughter will be joined to Jesus Christ in His saving death and glorious resurrection, original sin will be forgiven, and he or she will become a member of the Church. Baptism is the doorway to life in the Holy Spirit by which we are strengthened to live the life of grace and virtue. The baptism of your child has its own special preparation time, often known as pre-Jordan, and is something that your parish pastor can explain to you more fully.

QUESTIONS FOR PERSONAL REFLECTION OR DISCUSSION

1) What are some blessings that God has shared with you in your life?

2) The next time you pray, picture yourself speaking with Mary as she is "proceeding in haste" to visit her cousin, Elizabeth, and share her good news. What would you say to Mary? What would you want Mary to say to you?

3) What was the word or phrase in the prayer of blessing (the bold print on Pages 18-19) that spoke to your heart the most?

Shutterstock

Chapter Three

The Parish

The commitment to follow Christ takes extraordinary courage. In our world today there is much violence and hardship. It is not easy to follow the Lord Jesus. We need His strength in order to be His disciples. Every blessing we receive gives us strength to follow the Lord. The Rite for the Blessing of a Child in the Womb, while it brings abundant riches to the child and to his or her mother and father, is, as we discussed, also a *sign* for others. The blessing is *a moment of evangelization*, of spreading the Gospel of Jesus within the life and rhythm of the entire parish community. This is why the moment of new evangelization is enhanced by celebrations of the blessing during the celebration of holy Eucharist. The celebration of the blessing, perhaps on three or four separate times throughout a given calendar year, is a warm way to reach out to the mother and her family, and is a fruitful time to invite the family to baptismal preparation. The blessing opens, and can reopen, the "door of faith" (Acts 14:27).

The gift of your child has already begun to transform your life. You probably already have begun to "leave behind" the old ways — perhaps you get the rest you need now, you save financially for the future, you eat more healthily — and maybe you are even praying more, asking God to keep you and your child and family safe. The gift always longs to be shared further. While, as we discussed, the blessing can happen privately or with only a few people present, celebrating the blessing of the child in the womb in the midst of the Sunday Mass can really transform those who are present and have the privilege of sharing this moment of new life and joy.

The blessing of the child in the womb unites the parish. Adults face many fears and difficulties in the world. We don't often talk about it, but for all of our sophistication, we often can be easily bewildered and distressed. No matter how advanced we may consider ourselves, times of hurt and confusion easily slip into our lives - sometimes for a long period. The Lord Jesus himself is the answer.

Wittman

Jesus tells us very clearly, "whoever welcomes a child in my name, welcomes me" (Mk 18:5). As always, the simple words of Jesus have profound meaning. Jesus is well acquainted with the fragility, neediness, and innocence of the child. He especially knows the helpless vulnerability and utter dependence of the child in the womb. The LORD nonetheless sees the months in the womb as a precious and privileged time of His own immediate and irrevocable love for the child: "Before I formed you in the womb I knew you, before you were born I dedicated you" (Jer 1:5).

The LORD simply insists that we must become like little children to enter the kingdom of heaven (see Mk 10:15). The Holy Spirit longs to help us, as children of God, to cry out, "Abba, Father!" (Rom 8:15; Gal 4:6). "Abba" is the special word spoken by Jesus (Mk 14:36). It is the word of the child for the Father. Only with the strength and trust that comes from the LORD can we truly face the difficulties of everyday life. The Rite for the Blessing of a Child in the Womb is a great gift to the entire parish because the child always reminds us of the LORD Jesus and His love for us. The blessing of the child reminds all of us, no matter how grown up we may be, that we must always become children before God and entrust ourselves to His saving mercy.

Questions for Personal Reflection or Discussion

1) What is the particular strength you need right now in your life in order to be able to follow the Lord more closely? How does your parish community support you in your walk with the Lord?

2) What would be a good reason to have the Rite for the Blessing of a Child in the Womb during Sunday Mass?

3) What does Jesus mean when He says, "Whoever welcomes a child in my name welcomes me" (Mk 18:5)?

SHUTTERSTOCK

Chapter Four

Society

The celebration of the blessing of the child in the womb is a deeply personal moment, but it is not private. Your love for your child is important. Not only does the parish need to experience the blessing of this love, but so, too, does the world. In fact, the world sorely needs to understand in a new way the great gift of human life. The modern world around us moves very quickly. We can easily forget the beauty and awe of God's creation and the gift of new life.

There are many pressures that we face each day. It might be that work or school is very stressful. Being unemployed is even more filled with anxiety. Even our life at home may be unpredictable and hectic. The more progress we seek, the more pressure we find. As we sit in traffic, struggle to pay our bills, or shuffle along in the crowded mall, the natural wonder and amazement of the child can seem far away. Hope can seem far away. We can forget the importance of new life.

The child brings hope near. Society needs the child. The child reminds us of the deep immensity of love. The child helps each one of us and the world around us to become more childlike.

SHUTTERSTOCK

The child trusts in the love and security of his or her father and mother. The child lives in the same stressful world as we adults, yet the child sees the world as full of radical possibilities for joy, imagination, and love. The child has a special mission to help adults recapture a childlike spirit amidst our daily responsibilities.

There is another great gift that this blessing bestows not only on the child but also on the entire world. The blessing of the child in the womb reminds society to welcome, and to never reject, the child in the womb. The blessing is also a witness to the intrinsic dignity of human life from the very first moment of conception to natural death. The blessing can give society a fresh start on the road to respect and reverence for the gift of life.

Questions for Personal Reflection or Discussion

1) Why is it that a child brings hope?

2) What are the daily pressures that can sometimes prevent us from seeing God's gifts around us, especially the gift of new human life?

3) What would it mean for society to have reverence for all human life?